TRAIL OF COMMERCE AND CONQUEST

The End of the Trail, painting by Gerald Cassidy, *courtesy* Museum of New Mexico, Neg. No. 6977.

TRAIL OF COMMERCE AND CONQUEST

A Brief History of the Road to Santa Fe

JACK D. RITTENHOUSE

SANTA FE TRAIL ASSOCIATION
2000

Printed in the U.S.A.

Santa Fe Trail Association
PO Box 3
Woodston KS 67675

ISBN: 0-938463-03-9

The cover illustration is from Josiah Gregg's *Commerce of the Prairies*, 1844. The Frank A. Cooper map in the center is reproduced by permission of his widow, Velma Cooper Purdy, with gratitude.

FOREWORD TO 1987 PRINTING

IN 1971 Jack D. Rittenhouse published his celebrated *The Santa Fe Trail, A Historical Bibliography* (University of New Mexico Press) to help commemorate the one hundred and fiftieth anniversary of the opening of the Trail by William Becknell in 1821. As the author explained it, his book was intended to provide first aid to all readers, scholars, librarians, and book collectors making their way through the voluminous literature of the Santa Fe Trail.

To place his bibliography in perspective, Rittenhouse included a concise and well-crafted introduction representing a summary history of the Trail. It is that introduction, with some added material, that is now being issued separately by the Santa Fe Trail Council, under the title *Trail of Commerce and Conquest.*

With the growing interest in Trail studies, the Council thought it timely to bring out a short history that would give readers a quick and accurate overview of the subject. No such publication has been available since Stanley Vestal's little pamphlet, *Wagons Southwest,* went out of print thirty years ago. When Rittenhouse was approached, he graciously granted permission to the reprinting of his work in this new form, with all proceeds going to the use of the Council.

Although Michigan-born, Jack D. Rittenhouse has spent most of his life in the Southwestern states. He is well-known in literary circles as an author, editor, bibliographer, and publisher. For many years his prestigious Stagecoach Press turned out fine limited editions on regional history. His own writings have dealt with subjects ranging from horse-drawn vehicles to ghost towns. Now a bookseller, he can be classed as a member "in the thinning ranks of old-time Western Americana dealers."

The Santa Fe Trail Council was organized in September of 1986 during a Trail Symposium at Trinidad, Colorado. Its purpose is to encourage interest in Trail studies by sponsoring a variety of commemorative and educational activities. In the brief period since its founding, the Council has inaugurated a handsome newsletter, *Wagon Tracks*, and has initiated programs that have spotlighted the significant role of the Trail in our nation's history.

For more than a century, the dramatic story of the Santa Fe Trail has captivated the imagination of readers. It is therefore safe to predict that new generations of Americans will discover in this old tale a subject of endless fascination. For beginners on the Trail, a good place to start is with Rittenhouse's *Trail of Commerce and Conquest*.

Marc Simmons, Pres.
Santa Fe Trail Council

FOREWORD TO 2000 PRINTING

JACK D. Rittenhouse died August 10, 1991. It was his desire, conveyed by his widow, that *Trail of Commerce and Conquest* continue to be published by the Santa Fe Trail Association. The Santa Fe Trail Council, founded in 1986, changed its name to Santa Fe Trail Association in 1987 to avoid confusion with the Santa Fe National Historic Trail Advisory Council, created when the Santa Fe Trail was added to the National Historic Trails System in 1987.

Rittenhouse received an Award of Merit from the Santa Fe Trail Association in 1987 to give special recognition to his book, *The Santa Fe Trail, A Historical Bibliography,* the introductory chapter of which comprises this publication. Since first published in 1987, *Trail of Commerce and Conquest* has served as an introduction to Trail history for thousands of readers. It is now being printed again in order to keep a brief and inexpensive overview of the Santa Fe Trail available to new generations of Trail aficionados.

In 1993 the Santa Fe Trail Association, with the assistance of Ray Dewey of Santa Fe, New Mexico, established the Jack D. Rittenhouse Memorial Stagecoach Award, given biennially to honor the life work of a Santa Fe Trail scholar. This award includes a special Santa Fe Trail Blanket, courtesy of Dewey Trading Company, and $250. In this way the Association honors the late Jack Rittenhouse and perpetuates his devotion to Trail scholarship, as does the reprinting of this booklet.

The generosity of the Rittenhouse family is gratefully acknowledged. Special thanks are also extended to the Museum of New Mexico for permission to reproduce the illustration on the frontispiece, to the Kansas State Historical Society for the illustration "Fording the Arkansas," to the United States Army Military History Institute for the photograph of Kit Carson, to Velma Cooper Purdy for permission to reproduce the map in the centerfold, and to Holly Brumbaugh who did the typing for this edition. A few corrections have been made in brackets.

Readers who wish to know more about the Trail are invited to join the Santa Fe Trail Association. Membership includes a subscription to the quarterly, *Wagon Tracks*, and opportunities to become involved in local chapter activities along the historic route, attend the biennial Trail Symposium held at different Trail locations in odd-numbered years, and participate in the biennial Trail Rendezvous at Larned, Kansas, in even-numbered years. The Association also offers for sale a broad selection of books in print about the Trail, as well as maps, posters, musical recordings, and other items. For more information or to join, contact the Santa Fe Trail Association, Santa Fe Trail Center, RR 3, Larned KS 67550.

Leo E. Oliva, Editor
Santa Fe Trail Association

TRAIL OF COMMERCE AND CONQUEST

NEARLY every history of the Santa Fe Trail begins with the same incident. Down the dirt streets of Franklin, a backwoods Missouri village, four men rode in from the west on January 29, 1822. Any arrival being news, their coming brought people into the streets, but for men returning from a five months' trading expedition the packs lashed to their horses seemed pitifully small. Then one of the traders lifted high a small rawhide sack and slashed it open with a knife. A shower of Spanish silver coins fell glittering to the ground. Thus were the possibilities of the Santa Fe trade and the trail announced to a community that was short of coin and full of restless men looking for adventure and profit.

The leader of the party was William Becknell. He and his companions had left Missouri on September 1, 1821, reached Santa Fe on November 16, and sold their trade goods to eager buyers. Their success started a regular trade across the route, and the wagons never stopped rolling until the railroad reached Santa Fe in 1880.

The annals of the Santa Fe Trail are long and diverse. The cast of characters included men as different as Coronado and J. E. B. Stuart, physician Adolph Wislizenus and gun-runner Albert Speyer, California land baron John Sutter and New York newspaperman William Rideing. The action involved massacres by men both red and white; raids by men of the Texas Republic and the later Confederate States; small parties that vanished without trace and trains of a hundred wagons stalled in terrible blizzards; poor men trying to get through with one yoke of sick oxen, and great business firms such as Russell, Majors & Waddell. Riders along the Trail included governors, generals, archbishops, consumptives seeking health, and brides who blanched at teamsters' oaths. The tale contains enough adventure to fill a library, but adventure was only the color on the surface; below lay a deeper importance.

The Santa Fe Trail was a good deal more than a local route for trade; it provided access to a huge portion of the West and helped to shape the development of a quarter of a continent. As the first road to be surveyed west of Missouri, it set the initial pattern for roadbuilding across the West. As an avenue of commercial success and of information about the land and people of northern Mexico, it contributed to the expansionist doctrine of Manifest Destiny that led to war with Mexico. Expanding trade on the Trail brought the development of wagon freighting enterprises and stagecoach mail lines on a corporate scale never before conceived, using wagons of new and massive design. The problems of protecting Trail traffic from mobile Indian tribes initiated new national policies toward the Indians, brought into being new types of military units such as the U.S. Dragoons, and fostered the concept of satellite frontier forts served from great central supply depots. The Santa Fe Trail was in many ways a microcosm of westward expansion, and a study of its history is a study of much of the early frontier West.

This was all in the past, but that past is still close to those now alive. At points in northeastern New Mexico you can look out across a vista that appears today as it did to Coronado in 1541, to Pedro Vial in 1792, to Kit Carson in 1826, and to the wagonmasters of Alexander Majors in 1858. Frame your view properly and you will see not a house, a fence, or a sign of man's passing. Shift your view slightly and you can plainly see the remains of the old Trail, with so many variant ruts that the wide trace looks like a narrow field plowed a few summers ago.

Historians know that dates are only convenient bench marks on a map of time. In one sense it is correct to say that the Santa Fe Trail began with the 1821-22 expedition of Becknell and his men, but Becknell was not the first on the route; he was only the first to start regular commerce over an already beaten path. Who was the Leif Ericson of the Santa Fe Trail? Was it Coronado, who in 1541 crossed northeastern New Mexico into a corner of Kansas before he abandoned his dream and turned back? Or was it someone among scores of others between Coronado and Becknell who tried to cross this unknown midcontinent? As far back as 1695, before St. Louis or New Orleans existed, the Spanish governor in Santa Fe heard vague news of Frenchmen venturing near from the northeast. In 1714 a Frenchman named Etienne Veniard Sieur de Bourgmont traveled far enough up the Missouri to hear Indian tales of possible commerce with New Mexico.

In 1719 a Spanish expedition set out from Santa Fe to explore toward Missouri, and the following year the governor of New Mexico sent a military expedition northeast toward the Platte River, where French voyageurs were reported forming an alliance with the Indians. When the expedition was defeated, the Spaniards established a protective outpost at El Quartelejo pueblo on the plains. Each side was aware of the other, across the wide barrier of empty land.

The first trading expedition known to have reached Santa Fe arrived there empty-handed. Two Frenchmen, Pierre and Paul Mallet, with seven companions, lost their pack animals during a river crossing but went on to the provincial capital in 1739. The Mallet brothers were welcomed by the New Mexicans who, fifteen hundred rugged miles from their colonial capital in Mexico City, felt isolated and neglected, but Spanish officials, fearing the effects of trade with outsiders, ruled against it. Nevertheless, contraband was welcome and Spanish border guards could be bribed. In 1744 Jacques Velo (or Belleau or Bellot) got as far as Pecos Pueblo before he was arrested. Other Frenchmen reached Taos in 1748 to trade guns for mules, and next year brought three more Frenchmen: Louis Febre, Pierre Satren, and Joseph Michel Ravallo. One was from New Orleans, one from Quebec, and the third from a French post in Arkansas. Febre was a tailor and the others were carpenters. As Santa Fe had no artisans in either craft, all three settled down in the ancient city.

From this time on the visitors came in a stream. Felipe de Sandoval, a wanderer from Spain by way of Jamaica and New Orleans, arrived in 1750. Four more French traders came that same year, and their goods were seized and sold. In 1752 Jean Chapuis and Louis Feulli reached the mission at Pecos, and they too were imprisoned and their goods taken. In 1773 a Virginian, John Rowzee Peyton, was shipwrecked off the mouth of the Rio Grande and taken to Santa Fe as a prisoner. He escaped the following year and made his way overland to St. Louis, possibly by a route near that of the later Santa Fe Trail. In 1790 one of the French traders and scouts who were active along the upper Missouri River met Frenchmen who had been in New Mexico and eagerly questioned them about the possibility of trade with the province.

The first real trailblazer in the Southwest was Pedro Vial, a Frenchman in the employ of Spain. In

1786 he traveled from San Antonio northwest to Santa Fe, and about a year later he opened a similar trail from Santa Fe southeast to Natchitoches in Louisiana. In 1792 he was instructed to seek a route from Santa Fe to St. Louis and successfully completed this assignment. Vial deserves more credit that he has received.

These lonely venturings and random reconnoiterings may seem absurd to an impatient modern American who thinks he would simply have struck west or southwest without ado. He forgets the barriers then–not the puny border guard around the Spanish province, but the land itself. We have come to know that the land, the waters, and the sky determine much that man may do. Topography offers channels, fords, and gateways for those clever enough to find and use them but it also places great obstacles in their way. It was the nature of the land that isolated the market of New Mexico from the merchants of the east. Any understanding of the Santa Fe Trail and its trade must begin with an awareness of the land these men crossed.

From Santa Fe it is roughly seven hundred miles to San Antonio, nearly eight hundred miles to Kansas City, and about nine hundred miles to central Louisiana. On any of these journeys more than half the distance is across vast plains where in early days Indians were frequent and water was scarce. The first natural routes were the rivers, of which the three greatest in the region are the Missouri, the Arkansas, and the Red. The Missouri flows down through the Dakotas and Nebraska into Kansas, where, at modern Kansas City, it turns east to join the Mississippi near St. Louis. The Arkansas, middle of the three, leaves its snow-fed headwaters in Colorado and flows east along the lower edge of Kansas, making a great bend before it plunges southeast through Oklahoma and on to join the Mississippi in east central Arkansas. The Red, rising in northwest Texas and flowing southeast, played a negligible role in the Santa Fe trade.

It was convenient on the frontier to send cargoes coming down the Ohio, the Wabash, the Illinois, or the upper Mississippi to St. Louis, west along the Missouri to the site of Kansas City, then west-southwest across the Kansas prairies to meet the Arkansas at its great bend. From there traders could take either of two routes: they could go up the Arkansas on the "Mountain Branch" into Colorado and drop down into New Mexico through Raton Pass. Or they could follow the Arkansas a short distance and take the dry "Cimarron Cutoff" across the plains of northeastern New Mexico. As caravans moved westward, they found that the land became a great open plain cut by small streams. On the Cimarron route there was little firewood, little water. A man could make it that way if he knew the waterholes; the land was not true desert, but it was inhospitable and unknown.

Other parts of the West were unknown, and by the Louisiana Purchase in 1803 the United States acquired a great parcel of mystery to be explored. Lewis and Clark set out in 1804 to go up the Missouri and across to the Pacific. On their return in 1806, as they passed the Kansas region, they were told that it might be possible to go overland to trade with Mexico. They duly noted this fact in their records. Meanwhile, also in 1804, a Kaskaskia trader named William Morrison sent Jean Baptiste La Lande overland to New Mexico with a supply of trade goods. La Lande reached Santa Fe, sold his goods, liked the place, and stayed there. In 1805 another trader named James Purcell, sometimes recorded as Pursley, also got to Santa Fe and stayed.

Lewis and Clark had barely returned from the Far Northwest when a second expedition, led by Zebulon Pike, was sent to explore the Arkansas River to its source and return by way of the Red. Pike traveled along the Arkansas in 1806, making careful notes and maps as he went. Beyond the great bend of the river he traversed country that later was part of the Santa Fe Trail, and some authorities call him rather than Becknell the father of the Trail. When Pike reached the Rocky Mountains he turned south along them toward New Mexico. There he was taken into custody by the New Mexicans, who escorted him to Santa Fe (where he saw La Lande and Purcell) and on down to Chihuahua. He was released and made his way back to the United States in 1807, and in 1810 his book-length account of his journey was published in Philadelphia. This was the first report in English that described a possible route to Santa Fe, and there are indications that it soon was read by some Missourians.

While Pike was returning across Texas in 1807, Robert Fulton in the eastern part of the country was proving with his *Clermont* that river steamboats were practical. Fulton's invention would carry the goods down the Ohio and along the Missouri to the eastern end of the great Trail. It was also a great era of road building, with the construction of the Old National Road from Maryland to the Mississippi; the road continued as the Boon's Lick Trail across Missouri to the frontier settlements.

Encouraged by the success of Lewis and Clark, fur companies from St. Louis and the Boon's Lick country were soon extending their operations up the Missouri. From 1810 to 1840 the Mountain Men sent a flow of riches in furs back along the trails and rivers. In 1807 Jacques Clamorgan, a trader from St. Louis, made a successful trip overland to Santa Fe and went down to Chihuahua. He was perhaps the first truly successful Santa Fe trader.

In 1812-15 the U.S. was in another war and expeditions to the West had to wait. But trappers along the Missouri, such as Manuel Lisa, paid little heed to the war and still felt the lure of Santa Fe. Lisa wrote to the Spaniards, offering to trade, and in 1812 he sent Charles Sanguinet toward Santa Fe with a load of merchandise. Everything was lost to attacking Indians.

At about the same time a group of Missouri frontiersmen, perhaps encouraged by news of unrest in Mexico led by the priest Hidalgo, decided to make a try overland to New Mexico. Robert McKnight, James Baird, Samuel Chambers, and at least seven others reached Santa Fe. But Hidalgo had failed and the Spanish authorities remained implacable; they jailed the Americans and confiscated their goods. Not until 1821 was the last of the men, McKnight, released. Two other traders along the Arkansas, Auguste P. Chouteau and Jules de Mun, were seized and their good confiscated in 1817, but Jedediah Smith, one of the truly great pathfinders of the West, escaped this fate in 1818 when he guided a pack train over what would be the route of the Santa Fe Trail to the point where it met the Arkansas. His caravan was to meet a Spanish merchant at that point, near present Fort Dodge, but the trader failed to show up and Smith led the party back home.

Debates of these affairs in Congress produced a report that was probably the first congressional document to deal solely with the Santa Fe trade. And in 1819 the United States and Spain signed the Adams-Onís treaty, which, among other matters, defined the Arkansas River as the boundary between the two countries in the Southwest.

When the war of 1812 was concluded, the United States resumed its official exploration of the West. Lewis and Clark had gone northwest, Pike southwest; a third expedition, headed by Stephen H. Long, was sent in 1819 straight into the Rocky Mountains. It returned in 1820 along the Arkansas and produced another official report of that route.

Then came the landmark year of 1821. The records reveal several claimants for the honor of being "first" that year into Santa Fe. Samuel Adams Ruddock reached Santa Fe from Council Bluffs on June 8, on a trip to the Columbia River country. Jacob Fowler and Hugh Glenn, two Mountain Men, were trapping the beaver streams north of Santa Fe that year. William Becknell reached Santa Fe on November 16. And another trader, Thomas James, arrived there two weeks later.

Becknell, usually called Captain Becknell, and his companions took several pack animals loaded with Indian trade goods when they left the Missouri River. His intention apparently was to trade with the Indians, not to go to Santa Fe. But at the Mexican border he learned from Spanish dragoons that Mexico had asserted its independence from Spain and that U.S. traders would be welcome; so naturally he went on to Santa Fe. History was made with every peso that changed hands that day. It must have been a dry winter, because the Missourians made it back home in forty-eight days.

As soon as spring came in 1822, Becknell headed again for New Mexico, this time with at least three wagons, the first wheels to roll over the Trail. Jacob Fowler, coming down the Arkansas, noted in his wonderful journal that he saw the tracks of these wagons–an astonishing phenomenon at that time and place. Becknell and his party carried $3,000 worth of trade goods and made a profit of two thousand percent on their investment.

From these two expeditions led by Becknell comes the continuing disagreement over the year in which the Trail was opened. At its eastern end, in Franklin, Missouri, a tablet states the year was 1821, but at its western end, in Santa Fe, a bronze plaque says the Trail began in 1822. And the same difference of opinion appears in written accounts. No one disputes the facts; all agree that the Trail as a route of regular commerce was opened by William Becknell, that he wandered into Santa Fe with a pack train of Indian trade goods in 1821, and that he returned in 1822 with a few wagons. But they disagree on the interpretation of these facts.

Those who prefer 1821 may quote Max Moorhead, who refers to "the launching of this first successful trade in 1821," or they may point to Margaret Long's book about the Trail, which says flatly that "the Santa Fe Trail began at Franklin on the Missouri River in 1821." Others depend on Dean Earl Wood's unequivocal statement: "1821. That was the year of the origin of the Santa Fe Trail." But the group that is staunch for 1822 argues that Becknell's second trip was the first to carry goods intended for civilian–not Indian–trade, that it was the first to use wagons, and that it was the first to travel west over the Cimarron Cutoff route that became the main branch of the Trail. And the monuments erected along the Trail by the Daughters of the American Revolution, following decisions made in separate states, generally carried the 1821 date on markers in Missouri but used 1822 on markers in Kansas, Colorado, and New Mexico.

Two other experts, Josiah Gregg and William E. Brown, offer their readers a choice. In his first chapter, Gregg says, "During the year [1821] Captain Becknell . . . went out to Santa Fe by the far western prairie route," then adds when mentioning Becknell's second trip in 1822 that "it is from this period–the year 1822–that the virtual commencement of the Santa Fe Trail can be dated." Brown recognizes that Becknell reached Santa Fe in 1821 but continues, "Becknell's second expedition [in 1822] . . . was in fact the true beginning of the Santa Fe Trade."

It is the antiquarians who debate whether one should accept the "first" trip in 1821 or the "virtual commencement" and "true beginning" in 1822. Becknell himself may have provided a reasonable solution: he reached Santa Fe first on November 16, 1821, and arrived back in Missouri with packs of Spanish coin on January 29, 1822. So we may say that the Santa Fe Trail was opened in 1821-22, justifying a sesquicentennial in 1971-72.

Two other expeditions had gone to Santa Fe in 1822. One was headed by Colonel Benjamin Cooper, the other by James Baird and Samuel Chambers, who had been imprisoned on their trading venture about ten years earlier but were ready to try again. Caught in a snowstorm along the Arkansas near the Cimarron Crossing, Baird and Chambers stayed through the winter. Their pack animals died, and the traders dug holes in the earth, cached their goods, then went on to Taos for fresh mules and returned for the merchandise. The holes remained a gaping landmark known for years as The Caches.

In 1823 only one caravan, led by Stephen Cooper, left Missouri for Santa Fe, but in 1824 Trail commerce really began with a well-organized caravan of eighty men, using twenty-five wagons and a small field piece. The party was guided by Alexander Le Grand, an elusive figure who turns up at random places in the history of the Southwest. Also along were Augustus Storrs, who became U.S. consul at Santa Fe the next year, and M. M. Marmaduke, a future governor of Missouri. The caravan carried $35,000 in trade goods, and the trip was successful in every way.

Missouri had been admitted as a state in 1821, but she was in financial difficulties; her banks had failed and her people were on the brink of a barter economy for lack of hard money and any reliable paper currency. One of her first senators was Thomas Hart Benton, a man of energy and eloquence, then in his early forties. Benton saw that Missouri's hope lay in her strategic position as gateway to the West. William Ashley's fur trading company was operating up the Missouri in 1822; Jedediah Smith and Thomas Fitzpatrick had just discovered South Pass, opening up what would become the Oregon Trail; and Peter Skene Ogden had recently explored Great Salt Lake. These developments, together with the possibilities of the Santa Fe trade, pointed the way to the future for Missouri.

Benton became the champion of the West in Congress and remained so throughout his thirty years in the Senate. He now began pushing for development of the Santa Fe Trail, first asking Storrs and Marmaduke to send him information, which he had published as congressional documents. In March 1825 he carried a bill through Congress calling for a survey of the Trail, and before the year ended the survey party was at work in the field. The Santa Fe Trail was now a matter of national interest and no longer of importance to only a few frontier villages.

Diplomatic obstacles arose when the survey commissioners, headed by George Champlin Sibley, approached the Mexican border at the Arkansas. American frontiersmen considered the Trail a route of beneficial commerce and healthy enterprise, and the citizens of Santa Fe wanted badly the goods they hoped would come to them along the Trail. But the young government of Mexico viewed the Trail with serious misgivings. To them it was a potential military highway, a threat aimed straight at their northern border. Knowing that with merchandise would come also influence and the possibility of trouble, and that if trouble arose troops might use the Trail to protect U.S. interests, they felt the doubts and fears that had worried the Spanish viceroys in the days of the Mallet brothers and McKnight. But despite these misgivings, they eventually agreed to the survey.

The Sibley survey trip was more or less a fiasco. It

surveyed the route first to Taos instead of to Santa Fe. Strictly speaking, Taos was a port of entry to Mexico, but it was difficult for wagons to reach that village, and once there they could not be taken on to Santa Fe. So the survey party laid out a branch road to Santa Fe. It was all unnecessary, really, because the wagonmen already knew the route and took the shortest way. The details of Sibley's survey were not published for guidance of caravans at the time. A few mounds were erected to mark the route, but they soon disappeared. Nevertheless the survey produced two things of significance: more national publicity for the Trail, and the signing of a treaty with the Osage Indians at Council Grove in 1825, providing for a semblance of peace along part of the route. That treaty was one of the first steps toward an Indian policy in the West.

Caravans continued along the Trail each year. At this stage anyone could take part in the trade. A man had only to buy enough goods to load a wagon, and if he lacked that much cash himself he could borrow it or persuade friends to join him in backing the venture. The assorted wagons gathered at Council Grove in late spring and journeyed on together as one great annual caravan. With the caravan in 1826 a runaway apprentice named Christopher "Kit" Carson made his first journey to New Mexico.

In 1827 serious trouble began with the Indians. They had appeared frequently to demand gifts ever since the first wagons lumbered over the Trail, but in 1827 the Pawnee Indians attacked a group of returning traders and made off with a hundred head of mules and other livestock. The next year there were two caravans, both big and both successful. The leaders were returning with a thousand head of mules and horses and were near the present Oklahoma-New Mexico boundary when Indians crept up on the sleeping men, seized their guns, and shot two: Daniel Monroe and the

Christopher "Kit" Carson, *courtesy* U. S. Army Military History Institute, Carlisle Barracks, Pennsylvania.

son of Samuel McNees. Young [Robert] McNees died instantly; Monroe soon afterward. While the traders were burying their dead, a handful of curious Indians appeared on the opposite bank of the creek. Not knowing or caring whether these were the murderers, the enraged caravanners shot all but one, who escaped to tell his tribe. Thus began a bitter feud that was not ended for two generations. The traders journeyed on after gaining their immediate revenge, but they lost all of their livestock before reaching home.

Losing mules was the same as losing silver. In the first years of the Santa Fe trade, most of the hard money of New Mexico was carried to Missouri. That state, now recovered from its financial instability, had become known as the "hard money" state and Spanish coins circulated as readily as any other. Senator Benton became the champion of coin instead of paper money and was for years known as "Old Bullion." But mules were as good as money in Missouri. Before 1824 the records make no mention of mules in a state that later became nationally famous for them. The first ones came in over the Santa Fe Trail. Not until 1838 was jack-breeding stock brought in from the island of Malta. Until 1829 mules were used instead of oxen to draw the Trail wagons. And in all years the Indians preferred mules over coin as booty.

The deaths of Monroe and McNees, together with the loss of a thousand head of stock, threw a chill into Missouri traders. They demanded protection, and they got it–for a year. In 1829 Major Bennet Riley and an infantry escort accompanied the caravan as far as the Arkansas, *i.e.*, to the Mexican border. From there on a Mexican escort guarded the train to its destination.

By 1830 the Trail was well established between Independence, Missouri, and Santa Fe. The distance, reported variously in different accounts, was 775-780 miles. Because old accounts often tell of travelers starting from such places as Boon's Lick, Boonville, Arrow Rock, Franklin (Old or New), Blue Mills Landing, Fort Osage, Independence, Independence Landing, Westport, Cooper's Fort, Westport Landing, or Kansas (later Kansas City), a brief explanation is in order.

The Boon's Lick Trail leading west from St. Louis ended in a region known as the Boon's Lick Country, around the town of Franklin on the northeast bank of

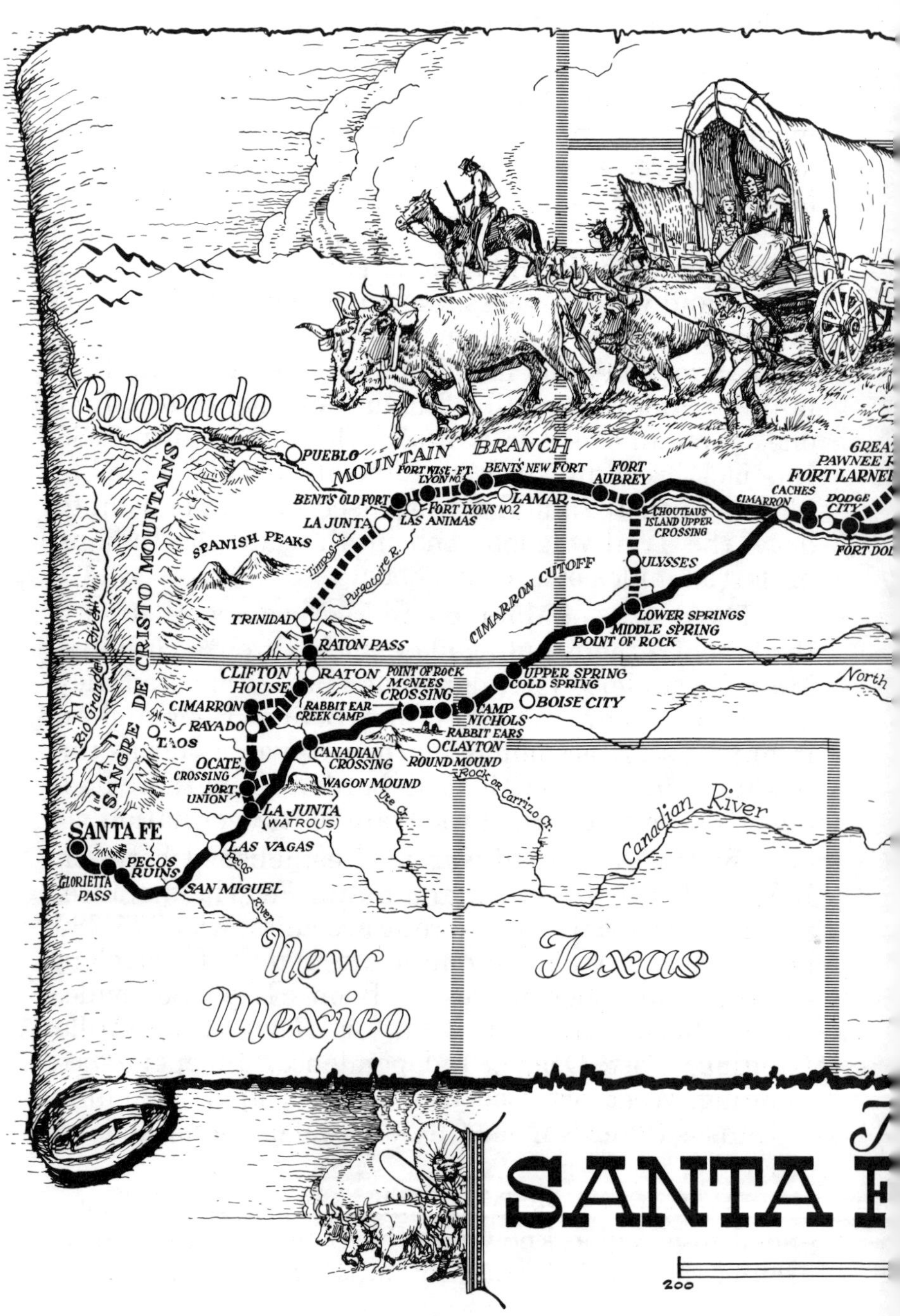

Colorado
PUEBLO
MOUNTAIN BRANCH
FORT WISE-FT. LYON NO.1
BENT'S NEW FORT
FORT AUBREY
BENT'S OLD FORT
LAMAR
FORT LYONS NO.2
LAS ANIMAS
LA JUNTA
CHOUTEAUS ISLAND UPPER CROSSING
CACHES
CIMARRON
DODGE CITY
SPANISH PEAKS
SANGRE DE CRISTO MOUNTAINS
Timpas Cr.
Purgatoire R.
CIMARRON CUTOFF
ULYSSES
TRINIDAD
LOWER SPRINGS
MIDDLE SPRING
POINT OF ROCK
RATON PASS
CLIFTON HOUSE
RATON
POINT OF ROCK
McNEES CROSSING
UPPER SPRING
COLD SPRING
CIMARRON
RABBIT EAR CREEK CAMP
CAMP NICHOLS
BOISE CITY
North
RAYADO
TAOS
RABBIT EARS
CLAYTON
Rio Grande River
CANADIAN CROSSING
ROUND MOUND
OCATE CROSSING
WAGON MOUND
Rock or Carrizo Cr.
FORT UNION
Ute Cr.
Canadian River
LA JUNTA (WATROUS)
SANTA FE
LAS VAGAS
PECOS RUINS
Pecos River
GLORIETTA PASS
SAN MIGUEL
New Mexico
Texas
SANTA

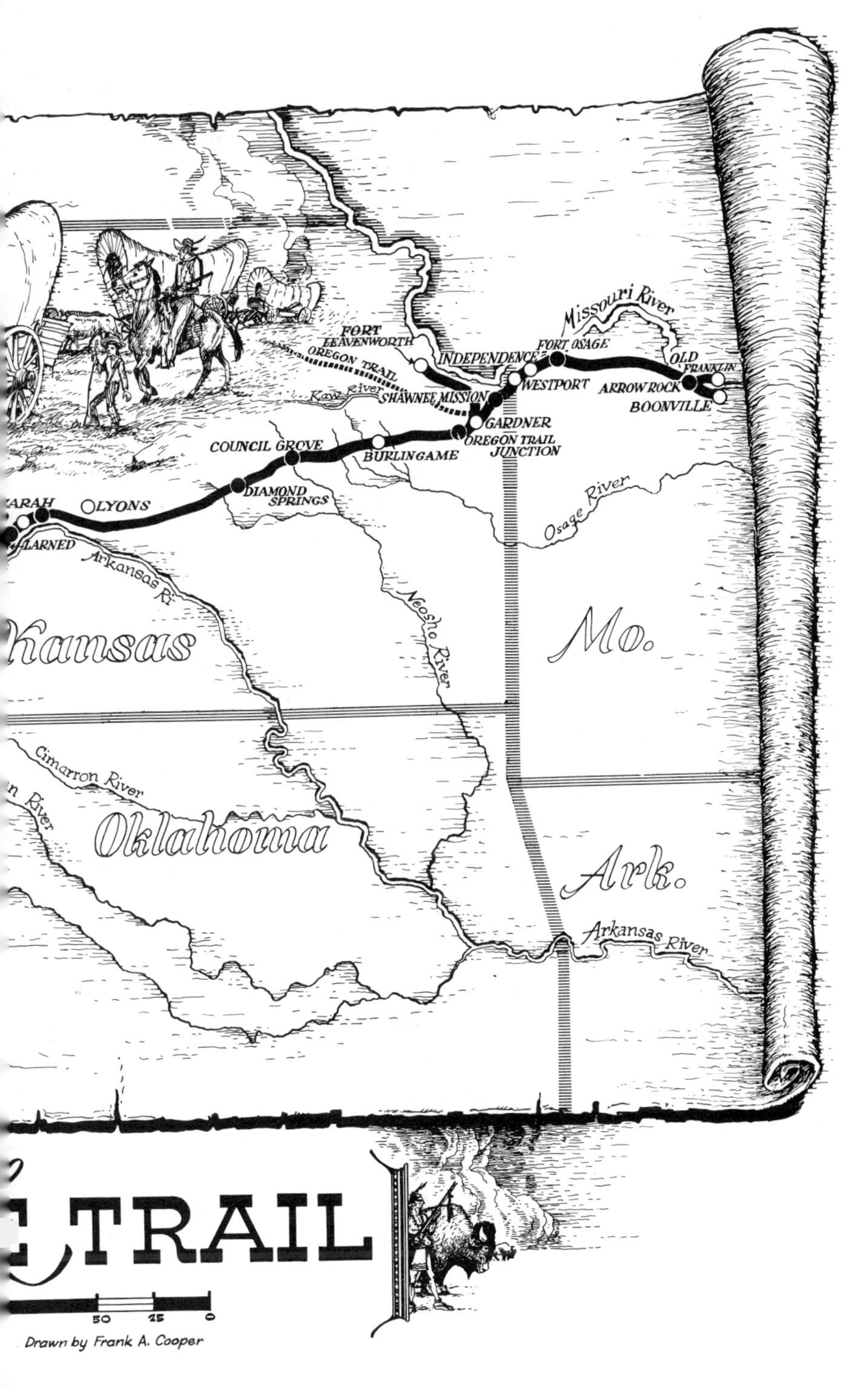

Drawn by Frank A. Cooper

the Missouri River. In 1828 a flood washed away most of the town and New Franklin was built two miles back from the river. From Franklin travelers usually crossed by ferry to Arrow Rock, or sometimes to Boonville a few miles below Arrow Rock. Thus Franklin (Old or New), Arrow Rock, Boonville, or the Boon's Lick Country were essentially the same point. Cooper's Fort was a few miles northwest of Franklin.

When steamboat navigation began on the Missouri, most cargoes were sent by boat along the river and the freight and passengers could go by water to Blue Mills Landing or Independence Landing, then south about three miles to the town of Independence, which became the eastern terminus of the Trail around 1827. By 1833 caravans could save another ten miles by having their cargoes set ashore at Westport Landing, ten miles beyond Independence Landing, then carted a few miles south to the town of Westport. Strictly speaking, Independence and Westport were not on the river but were served by their respective landings. In later years Westport Landing became the town of Kansas, later Kansas City, and the metropolis eventually absorbed Westport itself.

Actually, wagons came from many points on this turkey-track network, went on a hundred and fifty miles from Independence, and gathered to form the caravan or train at Council Grove. Along this initial stretch the wagons were joined at times by others coming down the side road from Fort Leavenworth, or they saw other companions depart where the Oregon Trail branched off from the Santa Fe Trail, about forty miles out of Independence. Before reaching Council Grove, travelers passed Round Grove and 110-Mile Creek (named for its distance along the Trail). Along this section the only obstacles were a few creeks and occasional quagmires. At Council Grove the main caravan was organized and all equipment was given a final check. There had been no town since Westport; the land lay empty ahead.

The Santa Fe Trail was an easy trail compared to the difficulties along routes such as those across the Sierra Nevada into California. The caravans would encounter sand hills, long dry stretches, steep creek banks, rocky fords, and narrow passes. By combining two or even three teams, wagonmen could struggle past the worst spots; with care in planning each day's march a camp could be made near water, along most sections.

Beyond Council Grove the grass was shorter; the wagons entered buffalo country as they passed Diamond Spring and Lost Spring, crossed Cottonwood Creek, and forded the Little Arkansas. Around every place name along the route there grew a dozen legends in the life of the Trail. About 270 miles from Independence the wagons came to the Arkansas River at the top of its great bend, and the Trail continued along the north bank of the river, past Pawnee Rock, Pawnee Fork, Coon Creek and The Caches, finally reaching the Middle Crossings near the present town of Cimarron, Kansas. It was approximately the halfway point.

At this point the caravans had a choice of routes: the Mountain Branch or the Cimarron Cutoff. The Mountain Branch was used during the Mexican War and the Civil War because it was safer from attack; later when the railroad was being built, wagons went from the end of track over the Mountain Branch, along the north bank of the Arkansas to Bent's Fort, then forded the river and continued on to Trinidad, over Raton Pass, down to the village of Cimarron and on to Ocate Crossing and Fort Union. During most of the commercial years of the Trail wagonmen preferred the shorter Cimarron Cutoff. With trains averaging only twelve to fifteen miles a day, any shortcut was

"Fording the Arkansas," *Harper's Monthly*, September 1862, *courtesy* Kansas State Historical Society.

important, so most wagons forded the Arkansas at the Middle Crossings.

Once across the river on the Cimarron Cutoff the trains encountered sand hills, and then came a sixty-mile waterless stretch, the worst on the Trail, known as the Jornada. At its end they reached the Cimarron River, which they followed across the present Oklahoma Panhandle, passing the Lower, Middle, and Upper Springs and entering New Mexico just before they came to McNees' Crossing. From there they wound past Rabbit Ear Camp, Round Mound, and Point of Rocks. The route became more rocky as they came to the Canadian River and turned southwest to Wagon Mound. Then there was a good stretch of plains again until they reached modern Watrous, where the Cimarron Cutoff and the Mountain Branch rejoined. Along this section in New Mexico, from McNees' Crossing to Watrous, the old ruts are best preserved, for the Trail was not just one pair of ruts but several. Wagons traveled two to four abreast, so they could form a corral quickly in case of attack. Consequently the Trail often resembles a trace drawn by the fingers of a giant hand dragged across the plain.

Traffic was heavier as the combined routes continued on from Watrous, past Las Vegas, Bernal Springs, San Miguel (where they forded the Pecos), past ruined Pecos Pueblo, and wound along Glorieta Pass through the mountains and over the last rocky climb to the slopes into Santa Fe.

By 1831 tourists were beginning to appear on the Trail. In that year Albert Pike, a writer from Arkansas, went over the route and wrote lyrical descriptions of it. And in the same year a great Mountain Man met his death on the Trail: Jedediah Smith, ready to settle down and turn merchant, wandered away from a night's camp and was killed by Indians.

At about this time a major change occurred in the

Santa Fe trade: it ceased to be an adventure for amateurs and became an occupation for businessmen. New Mexico was becoming glutted with ordinary trade goods, so that a man could no longer venture west with a few mirrors, needles, pans, and knives and sell them at tremendous profits. Prices began to drop while Mexican taxes rose; small traders were lucky to break even. Profits were possible only for operators of several wagons, using hired help, and studying the market carefully so that only desirable merchandise was hauled. Instead of selling a wagonload of goods in the plaza, the trader made advance arrangements to supply specific stores at the end of the route. Mexican taxes were levied per wagon, and this suggested the use of larger vehicles.

The buying of merchandise also changed. Instead of securing goods haphazardly from frontier shops in Missouri, traders now bought from large wholesale outfitters at Independence or Westport. Some even ordered from New York or other eastern centers or, a few years later, from Europe and had goods sent direct to a Missouri point. Of still greater importance was the increase in trade with Chihuahua. Long before the Santa Fe Trail opened, there had been a Spanish trade route down the Rio Grande and on south to Chihuahua. Operators in the Santa Fe trade now found they could take this route down to a new market in which there was demand for their goods and silver coins with which to pay for them. By 1840 half of all the Santa Fe Trail freight was continuing down to Chihuahua.

These changes were well along by 1831 when Josiah Gregg made his first Trail trip, for his health. He wrote undoubtedly the best contemporary account of the Trail and its trade, though he made only four round trips over the Trail before he left the trade in 1840. No student of the Trail can neglect Gregg's *Commerce of the Prairies*, published in 1844, but his description and statistics covered only the first twenty-two of the Trail's fifty-nine years; the adventure lay in the Gregg years, but the massive volume of trade and traffic came later.

The fur trade was reaching its peak around 1833. More and more men had been heading into the southern Rockies to bring out bundles of pelts. To accommodate the Mountain Men and trappers with supplies and to offer an outlet for their furs, Charles and William Bent, together with Ceran St. Vrain, built Bent's Fort on the upper Arkansas. This massive-walled adobe structure became a landmark on the Mountain Branch of the Trail and soon was a rendezvous for a group new to the frontier, the U.S. Dragoons.

The Dragoons were organized by order of President Jackson in 1833, because there was then no cavalry branch of the armed services and it had become evident that foot soldiers could not be effective in frontier warfare. The Dragoons were an elite corps of 1,832 men, at first commanded by Henry Dodge and later under such officers as Stephen Watts Kearny and Philip St. George Cooke. The men were mounted and could fight on horseback or on foot with sabre, carbine, and bayonet. The tactics they worked out in their first thirteen years and the manuals written for their use laid the groundwork for cavalry operations in the Mexican War, the Civil War, and the Indian wars.

In 1834 a detachment of Dragoons under Captain Clifton Wharton escorted a caravan along the Santa Fe Trail, the first such escort since Bennet Riley's service in 1829, and there were no more Dragoon escorts until 1843. But in 1835 the Dragoons made a long tour to present a show of force to the Indians of the West. The troopers rode north to the Platte River, followed it west to the Rocky Mountains, turned south down the eastern flank of those ranges to the Arkansas, then rode back along the Arkansas past Bent's Fort and over the Santa Fe Trail to their base at Fort Leavenworth.

A year later, in 1836, the Republic of Texas declared its independence from Mexico and defeated General Santa Anna at the Battle of San Jacinto. This portentous action had no immediate effect on the Santa Fe trade, although it tended to chill Mexican officials toward all Anglos, as U.S. citizens were called regardless of their color.

The Santa Fe trade continued to grow, despite Indian attacks such as those of the Pawnee in 1837 on a Bent, St. Vrain & Company train. In 1838 cost-conscious traders petitioned Congress for a free port of entry in Missouri. They asked that customs duties paid on imported goods landed in Atlantic ports and destined for the Mexican trade should be repaid by debenture or "drawback" when those bales and cases left Missouri in their original sealed condition. Seven years later this relief was granted.

Joseph Murphy, a St. Louis wagonmaker, was building bigger wagons for Trail use by 1840. The initial simple country wagons had long since given way to the "Pittsburgh" wagon, a variation of the old Conestoga, but Murphy's new vehicles were juggernauts. Their wheels were seven feet high, with rims eight inches wide, the wagon tongue was fifty feet long, and the bed was so deep that a man standing inside barely exposed the top of his head. The payload was from two to three tons.

The mounting traffic of these great wagons soon became a matter of economic interest to the Texas Republic. Texas had claimed the Rio Grande as a boundary, placing the eastern half of New Mexico, including Santa Fe, within the young republic. This claim was not recognized by Mexico, and in 1841 Texas sent out the Texan-Santa Fe Expedition to secure the political, military, and commercial control of Santa Fe.

More than three hundred men, calling themselves the Santa Fe Pioneers, left central Texas with twenty-one ox-drawn wagons laden with merchandise and a supply of political handbills. In the group were George Wilkins Kendall, Thomas Falconer, and Franklin Coombs, all of whom later wrote narratives of the trip.

The expedition, often misinformed by its guides, moved slowly over an erratic course. By the time its advance party reached New Mexico, near present Tucumcari, the men were suffering from thirst and hunger. The Mexican governor, Manuel Armijo, aware of their approach and naturally incensed about it, sent out detachments who induced the Texans to surrender. They were then marched south to Mexico and prison, from which most of the men were released the next year.

Despite the immediate futility of the Texan-Santa Fe Expedition, it had profound effects on trade along the Santa Fe Trail in the years that followed. One consequence was the Snively Expedition. In January 1843 a Texan named Jacob Snively petitioned the Republic of Texas for permission to form a new expedition that would intercept and seize the goods of Mexican traders along the portion of the Santa Fe Trail–nearly three hundred miles along the Cimarron Cutoff–that lay within the territory claimed by Texas. The Republic authorized Snively's expedition with certain qualifications: the force was not to exceed three hundred men; all actions were to be undertaken as in honorable warfare; and all goods seized were to be divided equally between the Texas government and the Snively Men.

At the same time a similar pro-Texan force, headed by Charles A. Warfield, was formed in northern New Mexico. The Warfield Expedition included several Mountain Men, among them Rufus Sage. Snively's men moved north and Warfield's group marched east, heading for a rendezvous on the Santa Fe Trail just below the Arkansas. They were aware that the land north of the river was U.S. territory. At the end of May 1843 Warfield's men disbanded after a desultory and fruitless campaign and some of them, including Warfield, joined Snively. A few weeks later the Snively forces met a Mexican detachment in a short but decisive battle in which seventeen Mexican soldiers were killed. But the spoils of victory were meager, and the Snively command broke into separate detachments.

Philip St. George Cooke, then a captain in the Dragoons, was commanding a caravan escort at this time along the Trail above the Arkansas. His troops were on the alert because a Mexican trader, Antonio José Chávez, had been killed near the site of today's Emporia [Lyons], in Kansas. Chávez' death had been blamed on Warfield's men, but it may have been the work of freebooters. Cooke moved rapidly south of the Arkansas to Snively's camp and ordered the Texans disarmed. The expedition then returned home and was disbanded. Enraged by the death of its soldiers and the killing of Chávez, the Mexican government placed a ban on all foreign traders coming overland into Mexico, but in response to an immediate outcry from Mexican citizens deprived of incoming goods the ban was soon lifted.

While Snively, Warfield, and Cooke were engaged in their encounters, John C. Frémont, on his Second Expedition to explore the Far West, traversed the Santa Fe Trail for the first time, following it along the Arkansas as far as Bent's Fort before heading on west. Two years later, on his Third Expedition, he used the Trail again and paused at Bent's Fort long enough to send young Lieutenant James Abert on a reconnaissance trip down through Raton Pass and on a wide loop eastward through the Canadian River country. Frémont went on to California and there became involved in the Bear Flag revolt against Mexican rule, and in 1846 young Abert was back through Raton Pass with a column of United States troops. Mexico's earlier fears that the Santa Fe Trail might be an avenue of conquest had become reality.

Expansionist fever had been rising in the United States for some years. The great migration westward over the Oregon Trail had begun in 1842-43 and was soon in full spate, and to the rallying cry of "54° 40' or Fight" for the Far Northwest were added less noisy but equally intense ambitions for the annexation of lush California. Then in 1845 Texas was admitted to the Union, transferring to the nation her claim to the Rio Grande boundary which Mexico disputed. If President Polk could not achieve peaceful acquisition of the desired territories, war seemed bound to come.

Tension was high and debate fierce as the year 1846 began, but in New Mexico affairs were progressing normally. The spring trade over the Trail topped the million dollar mark. Then on May 13 Congress declared war with Mexico.

The major thrust and the first battles of the war occurred in South Texas, but United States forces also moved along the Santa Fe Trail into New Mexico. Stephen Watts Kearny organized the Army of the West at Fort Leavenworth and led it to the Arkansas and thence along the Mountain Branch of the Trail because, although this route was a hundred miles longer than the Cimarron Cutoff, it had more water and also Bent's Fort to be used as a staging area. Francis Parkman, returning from the Northwest, met the advancing troops along the Arkansas, and just ahead of them journeyed another visitor who later wrote about the West, Adolph Wislizenus, who was taking a pleasure trip along the Santa Fe Trail. He was with a caravan that included a trader, Albert Speyer, whose wagons carried a cargo of fine Mississippi rifles ordered by Mexico. They managed to get to Chihuahua ahead of the troops, but other traders following Speyer were scooped up by Kearny's advancing men.

The troops left Bent's Fort in early August and marched over Raton Pass, down to Las Vegas, and on to Santa Fe. They expected to meet Mexican resistance in every canyon, every village, and at every ford, but encountered none anywhere. Governor Armijo had ordered a retreat from his prepared position. On August 19 Kearny, now a brigadier-general, proclaimed in Santa Fe the United States' occupation of New Mexico.

Reinforcements came along the Trail to strengthen the Army of the West. Included was the Mormon Battalion, an unusual unit that had been recruited from the great Mormon throng then encamped in Iowa on their way west. The United States government had promised to lend any possible financial aid in this Mormon migration, and the Mexican War offered an opportunity to redeem this pledge. Arrangements were made for a battalion of five hundred Mormons to accompany the Army of the West on its march to California; the wages of the men would aid their families, and the men themselves would reach the Pacific Coast.

When the Mormon Battalion, under Philip St. George Cooke, arrived at Santa Fe, a small group of men, feeling they were physically incapable of continuing the march, turned back over Raton Pass and set up a winter camp at what it is now Pueblo, Colorado. Kearny led part of the Army of the West on across Arizona to fight in California, and Cooke and the Mormon Battalion followed him. Another large part of the Army of the West, under Colonel Alexander Doniphan, marched down the Rio Grande to capture Chihuahua. Sterling Price, later a Confederate commander in Missouri, stayed behind as the military commander in Santa Fe.

Throughout this campaign, traffic on the Trail was heavy as Missouri teamsters trundled great loads of supplies across the plains. Many men who otherwise might never have entered the Santa Fe trade came to know the Trail during the war and in the years that followed became major operators along its route. The end of the war, with the signing of the Treaty of Guadalupe Hidalgo in 1848, initiated the busiest thirty-two years of the Trail's life. Increasing quantities of supplies were needed for the garrisons at Santa Fe and other military posts in the Southwest. In 1848 James Brown secured the first government contract to haul supplies from Fort Leavenworth to New Mexico, and contract freighting became a major enterprise across the plains. Brown formed a partnership with John Russell, and in 1850 a hundred-wagon Brown & Russell train, trying desperately to get late supplies into Santa Fe before the full winter set in, was caught in deep snow in New Mexico. Brown went to Santa Fe and got more teamsters and animals but died soon afterward from the exposure.

Others were using the Trail in these years, some with unusual experiences. In 1848 young François X. Aubry, an enterprising freighter, made an unbelievable ride to win a wager. In September, using a relay of mounts, he rode from Santa Fe to Independence on horseback, covering more than 750 miles in five days and sixteen hours. And between late April and mid-September 1849 some 2,500 persons took the Santa Fe route to the California gold fields in order to avoid any risk of cholera. Mountain Man Jim Kirker guided one of the California caravans as far as Santa Fe.

With the passing of the fur trade and increasing preference for the Cimarron route, activity at Bent's Fort declined; so William Bent burned the grand old landmark and built a new post farther down the

Arkansas. His brother Charles, who had moved to New Mexico, became the governor, and was killed at Taos during a wartime uprising in 1847.

Indian attacks still plagued traders and travelers on the Trail. At Point of Rocks in New Mexico, a physician named J. M. White and his family were killed, and at Wagon Mound in 1850 a ten-man party of mail carriers were killed and their mail scattered. For more than a hundred years treasure hunters have potholed the area in search of valuables that the mail was said, probably fictitiously, to contain.

When the Mexican War began, there was no U. S. fort except Leavenworth to serve the Santa Fe Trail, but with the increase in traffic and settlement that followed the war a series of forts were built. Altogether nineteen western forts were involved in the history of the Trail.

The oldest was the Spanish presidio at Santa Fe, established in 1610-11. In 1846 it was occupied by Kearny's troops, who promptly built a better defense a few hundred yards away and named it Fort Marcy. The second oldest fort was Fort Cavagnolle, built by the French in 1744 or 1745 at or near present Kansas City as part of a French plan to develop trade with Santa Fe. It was abandoned before 1760. Fort Osage was built on the northeast side of the Missouri River not far from Franklin in 1808. George C. Sibley in his survey of the Santa Fe Trail used Fort Osage as milepost zero. In 1827 Fort Osage was replaced by Fort Leavenworth as the major post at the eastern end of the Trail. Leavenworth was not located precisely on the Trail but was joined to it by a short military road.

During the Mexican War a post was needed midway between Fort Leavenworth and Fort Marcy, so Fort Mann was built in 1847-48, about eight miles west of present Dodge City. It was abandoned in 1850 when Fort Atkinson was built nearby. Fort Atkinson, predecessor of Fort Dodge and not to be confused with other forts named Atkinson in Nebraska and North Dakota, was first called Camp Mackay and then Fort Sumner; it became Fort Atkinson in 1851 and was abandoned in 1853.

In 1851 Fort Union was established astride the Santa Fe Trail east of Las Vegas, New Mexico. Before it was abandoned in 1891, its location was twice changed slightly. Fort Union became the principal supply and staging center for all military operations in the Southwest and was the hub of a great network of forts in Texas, New Mexico, and parts of Colorado, Kansas, and Arizona. Fort Leavenworth and Fort Union were linked by the Santa Fe Trail as their lifeline through all the Indian wars. Near Fort Union was a non-military trading post named Fort Barclay, built around 1849 by Alexander Barclay. He had been an employee of Bent and built his smaller fort on the model of old Bent's Fort.

In 1853 Fort Riley was built in Kansas. While not on the Santa Fe Trail itself, this fort–together with Leavenworth–provided troops who served along the Trail. In 1859 Fort Larned was built on the Trail in Kansas. First called [Camp on Pawnee Fork and] Camp Alert, then renamed Larned in 1860, it was closed in 1878. Within sight of Bent's New Fort on the Arkansas the Army in 1860 erected a post at first called Fort Fauntleroy [no, Fauntleroy was another post in New Mexico], then Fort Wise and finally Fort Lyon. It is usually referred to as Fort Lyon I.

When the Civil War opened, the existing chain of forts serving the Santa Fe Trail included Leavenworth, Riley, Larned, Lyon I, Union, and Marcy. Before that war ended at Appomattox, the campaigns to control the Indians in the West had already started. Between 1864 and 1867 several smaller posts were built along the Trail to aid in these campaigns.

In 1864 Fort Harker, at first called Fort Ellsworth, was built near present Ellsworth, Kansas. It lasted until 1878 [1873]. Also in 1864 Fort Zarah was built on the trail near present Great Bend, Kansas. It was closed in 1869. In 1865 Fort Dodge, Fort Aubry, and Camp Nichols were built. Fort Dodge, near present Dodge City, was a major post that lasted until 1882. Fort Aubry was a sod-house post built near present Kendall, Kansas; it lasted barely a year. Camp Nichols was built by Kit Carson along the Cimarron Cutoff where it nicks the edge of the present Oklahoma Panhandle, west of Boise City. It lasted only through a single summer. Both Aubry and Nichols were intended to be only temporary posts for short campaigns. In 1866 Fort Stevens was planned near Spanish Peaks in Colorado, not far from the northern end of Raton Pass, but the plans were cancelled before the fort was built. The last fort along the Trail was Fort Lyon II, built in 1867 near the first Fort Lyon. It was not closed until 1889.

Such a network of military posts needed a flood of supplies, and this opened the way for more rich contracts in government freighting. At the same time the government was beginning its surveys for railroads through the West. In 1853 two survey parties made the first leg of their trips over the Santa Fe Trail. John Gunnison's expedition sought one possible route through the Rockies, and the other expedition was that of E. F. Beale and Gwinn Harris Heap.

In that same year Alexander Majors began his wagon freighting operations along the Trail, and five years later he joined with two other wagonmen to form the famous firm of Russell, Majors & Waddell. Their name has been linked most prominently with the Pony Express, which never used the Santa Fe Trail, although Majors may have conceived his idea after seeing the postal couriers who carried dispatches over the Trail. By 1854 mail contracts were being awarded for two trips a month. Hockaday & Hall won the contract that year, away from David Waldo, who had held the contract since 1850 for mail carried once a month. Passenger stage lines began with the mail contracts. The Mexicans, whose role in freighting along the Trail has never been told adequately, were also active as freighters or outfitters during the entire life of the route. Names such as Manuel Escudero, Francisco Elguea, Francisco Perea, Antonio José Chávez, and Miguel Antonio Otero were among the most prominent on the Trail, and there were hundreds of Mexican teamsters with outfits small and large.

When the gold rush to Colorado started in 1858, the first groups headed west over the familiar Santa Fe route, and by the following year five hundred wagons a day were using the Trail to get to the new El Dorado. Later more direct routes through central Kansas to the Colorado camps lessened this traffic on the Santa Fe Trail. But freight volume continued to grow. In 1858 some $3,500,000 in goods was carried over the Trail, and by 1859 the volume had passed $10,000,000.

Then came the Civil War. Although the conflict between proslavery and antislavery forces had torn Kansas apart, it had little effect along the Trail, and at first the Civil War produced little activity there. "Buffalo Bill" Cody, scouting along the route for the 9th Kansas Cavalry, found only Indians. But before long the Confederates invaded New Mexico from Texas. Their first thrust carried them up the Rio Grande to capture the town of Mesilla and Fort Fillmore, and early in 1862 Brigadier General Henry H. Sibley took command of the Texans and fought his way north to take Santa Fe. His next goal was the seizure of Fort Union, with its great warehouses full of military supplies. When Colorado sent its 1st Regiment of Volunteers south through Raton Pass and along the

Santa Fe Trail to Fort Union, the opposing small armies met late in March in Glorieta Pass on the Trail a few miles east of Santa Fe. The battle was a draw; each side retired confident that it had won. But the Union forces had sent a detachment around to the south to destroy the Confederate supplies, and the Texans found themselves unable to renew the fight the nest day; they could only retreat homeward. The Civil War in the West was ended. Confederate guerrillas under William C. Quantrill occasionally attacked Union supply trains in eastern Kansas, with Dick Yeager leading the major forays, and similar groups under James Reynolds and Joel McKee were active along the Arkansas. In October 1864 the Battle of Westport, often called the "Gettysburg of the West," was fought in Missouri, but it was not a struggle solely for control of the Trail. General Sterling Price commanded the Confederate troops in this engagement, the largest west of the Mississippi. His defeat ended the fighting in the trans-Mississippi area.

During the war there was no loss in commerce. In 1862 $40,000,000 in goods and supplies went over the Trail in three thousand great wagons, compared to $450,000 in 230 wagons during 1843, the best year reported by Josiah Gregg. And the 1862 record was toppled when more than five thousand wagons moved over the Trail in 1866. In that year a former Mountain Man named Richens Lacy "Dick" Wootton hacked a better pass across Raton Pass and turned it into a profitable toll road.

The tremendous increase derived in part from a wave of population moving westward, from growth in both demand and wealth in New Mexico, and from the broadening campaign against the Indians, which resulted in more forts and more troops to be supplied. Some of these new soldiers in 1864 were the "Galvanized Yankees," Confederate soldiers who had been captured and then released on condition that they fight for the Union side in the West. Supplies were needed also for the Navajo and other tribes interned in the Bosque Redondo camp below Fort Union.

But the end of the Santa Fe Trail was in sight. In 1866 the Kansas-Pacific Railroad reached Topeka, and the Atchison, Topeka & Santa Fe Railway was soon to start. The town of Abilene, Kansas, sprang into existence in 1867 as one of the first cowtowns, and the great herds began moving north from Texas to the railroads. The Kansas-Pacific reached Kit Carson, Colorado, in 1870, and three years later the Atchison, Topeka & Santa Fe was extended to Granada, Colorado, not far from the northern entrance to Raton Pass. The Cimarron Cutoff section of the Trail was already almost completely abandoned by wagon traffic; wagons and stagecoaches only shuttled back and forth between the end of the tracks and Santa Fe. After a six-year lull the last excitement occurred along the Trail as rival rail lines fought to be first through Raton Pass. The Atchison, Topeka & Santa Fe won and spilled down onto the plains and into Las Vegas. On February 9, 1880, the first train steamed into Santa Fe. The Santa Fe Trail was ended as a freight route. But some who saw the last freight wagons lived to see also the first motor cars as tourists took over the old Trail as a scenic route, and when the Daughters of the American Revolution began to erect markers along the Trail after 1906, they were guided by men who could point to spots they personally remembered.

MILEAGE AND STOPS ON THE SANTA FE TRAIL, CIMARRON ROUTE

From Josiah Gregg's *Commerce of the Prairies.*

Independence to	MILES	TOTAL
Round Grove	35	
Narrows (Wakarusa Point)	30	65
110-Mile Creek	30	95
Bridge Creek	8	103
Big John Spring	40	143
Council Grove	2	145
Diamond Spring	15	160
Lost Spring	15	175
Cottonwood Creek	12	187
Turkey Creek	25	212
Little Arkansas	17	229
Cow Creek	20	249
Arkansas River (Big Bend)	16	265
Walnut Creek (up Arkansas)	8	273
Ash Creek	19	292
Pawnee Fork	6	298
Coon Creek	33	331
Caches	36	367
Ford of the Arkansas	20	387
Sand Creek (leave Arkansas River)	50	437
Cimarron River (Lower Spring)	8	445
Middle Spring of the Cimarron	36	481
Willow Bar	26	507
Upper Spring	18	525
Cold Spring (leave Cimarron River)	5	530
McNees Creek	25	555
Rabbit Ear Creek	20	575
Round Mound	8	583
Rock Creek	8	591
Point of Rocks	19	610
Rio Colorado (Canadian River)	20	630
Ocate	6	636
Santa Clara Spring	21	657
Rio Mora	22	679
Rio Gallinas (Las Vegas)	20	699
Ojo De Bernal	17	716
San Miguel	6	722
Pecos Village	23	745
Santa Fe	25	770

MILEAGE AND STOPS ON THE SANTA FE TRAIL, MOUNTAIN ROUTE

From the *Junction City Union*, August 4, 1866.

Junction City to	MILES	TOTAL
Chapman's Creek	11	
Abilene	13	24
Sand Spring	3	27
Salina	22	49
Pritchard's	14	63
Fort Ellsworth	16	79
Well's Ranch, Plum Creek	18	97
Fort Zarah	23	120
Fort Larned	31	151
Rock Hollow	9	160
Big Coon Creek	15	175
Aroyo Blanco	16	191
Little Coon Creek	4	195
Fort Dodge	11	206
Cimarron Crossing	25	231
Pawnee Forts	21	252
Lone Tree	9	261
Bluffs	10	271
Chouteau Island	20	291
Fort Aubrey	16	307
Fair View	9	316
Pretty Encampment	11	327
Bluff at head of Salt Bottom	19	346
Sand Creek	10	356
Fort Lyon	19	375
Twelve mile point	23	398
Little Sand Creek	5	403
Bent's Old Fort	6	409
Big Aroyo	21	430
The Mounds	9	439
Iron Spring	10	449
Hole in Rock	14	463
Hole in Prairie	15	478
Gray's Ranche	19	497
Trinidad	4	501
Summit of Raton Pass	15	516
Red River	14	530
Vermejo Creek	23	553
Maxwell's	12	565

	MILES	TOTAL
Ryado	10	575
Murray's	9	584
Apache Hill	8	592
Ocate Creek	6	598
Fort Union	17	615
Las Vegas	26	641
Tecojole [Tecolote]	12	653
San Jose	15	668
Pecos	20	688
Pigeon's Ranche	5	693
Johnson's Ranche	6	699
Santa Fe	13	712

RECOMMENDED READING

Sam Arnold, *Eating Up the Santa Fe Trail* (Boulder: University Press of Colorado).

William Y. Chalfant, *Dangerous Passage: The Santa Fe Trail and the Mexican War* (Norman: University of Oklahoma Press).

W. W. H. Davis, *El Gringo: New Mexico and Her People* (Lincoln: University of Nebraska Press).

Robert L. Duffus, *The Santa Fe Trail* (Albuquerque: University of New Mexio Press).

Jane Lenz Elder & David J. Weber, eds., *Trading in Santa Fe: John M. Kingsbury's Correspondence with James Josiah Webb, 1853-1861* (Dallas: SMUPress).

Mark L. Gardner, *Bent's Old Fort NHS* (Tucson: Southwest Parks & Monuments Association).

Mark L. Gardner, *Brothers on the Santa Fe and Chihuahua Trails* (Boulder: University Press of Colorado).

Mark L. Gardner, *Santa Fe Trail, National Historic Trail* (Tucson: Southwest Parks & Monuments Association).

Lewis H. Garrard, *Wah-to-Yah and the Taos Trail* (Norman: University of Oklahoma Press).

Josiah Gregg, *Commerce of the Prairies* (Norman: University of Oklahoma Press).

Kate L. Gregg, ed., *The Road to Santa Fe* (Albuquerque: University of New Mexico Press).

Thomas B. Hall, *Medicine on the Santa Fe Trail* (Arrow Rock: Friends of Arrow Rock).

David Lavender, *Bent's Fort* (Lincoln: University of Nebraska Press).

Susan Shelby Magoffin, *Down the Santa Fe Trail and into Mexico* (Lincoln: Univeristy of Nebraska Press).

Gene and Mary Martin, *Trail Dust: A Quick Picture History of the Santa Fe Trail* (Boulder: Johnson Publishing Company).

Marian Meyer, *Mary Donoho: New First Lady of the Santa Fe Trail* (Santa Fe: Ancient City Press).

Max L. Moorhead, *New Mexico's Royal Road: Trade and Travel on the Chihuahua Trail* (Norman: University of Oklahoma Press).

W. B. Napton, *Over the Santa Fe Trail, 1857* (Arrow Rock: Friends of Arrow Rock).

Leo E. Oliva, *Fort Dodge: Sentry of the Western Plains* (Topeka: Kanas State Historical Society).

Leo E. Oliva, *Fort Larned: Guardian of the Santa Fe Trail* (Topeka: Kansas State Historical Society).

Jami Parkison, *Path to Glory: A Pictorial Celebration of the Santa Fe Trail* (Kansas City: Highwater Editions).

Marian Russell, *Land of Enchantment* (Albuquerque: University of New Mexico Press).

Marc Simmons, *Following the Santa Fe Trail: A Guide for Modern Travelers* (Santa Fe: Ancient City Press).

Marc Simmons, *The Old Trail to Santa Fe* (Albuquerque: University of New Mexico Press).

Marc Simmons, *On the Santa Fe Trail* (Lawrence: University Press of Kansas).

David K. Strate, *West by Southwest: Letters of Joseph Pratt Allyn, A Traveller Along the Santa Fe Trail, 1863* (Dodge City: Kansas Heritage Center).

John E. Sunder, ed., *Matt Field on the Santa Fe Trail* (Norman: University of Oklahoma Press).

Henry P. Walker, *The Wagonmasters: High Plains Freighting from the Earliest Days of the Santa Fe Trail to 1880* (Norman: University of Oklahoma Press).

Dave Webb, *Santa Fe Trail Adventurs: An Activity Book* (Dodge City: Kansas Heritage Center).

James J. Webb, *Adventures in the Santa Fe Trade, 1844-1847* (Lincoln: University of Nebraska Press).